WRITERS REPUBLIC

JASON LANG

and the iTunes Scandals

THE REAL-LIFE STORY ABOUT
THE GILGO BEACH MURDERS
AND THE CRAIGSLIST RIPPER

JASON LANG

WRITERS REPUBLIC L.L.C.
515 Summit Ave. Unit R1
Union City, NJ 07087, USA

Website: *www.writersrepublic.com*
Hotline: *1-877-656-6838*
Email: *info@writersrepublic.com*

Ordering Information:
Quantity sales. Special discounts are available on quantity purchases by corporations, associations, and others. For details, contact the publisher at the address above.

Library of Congress Control Number:	2022908914	
ISBN-13:	979-8-88536-218-4	[Paperback Edition]
	979-8-88536-219-1	[Hardback Edition]
	979-8-88536-220-7	[Digital Edition]

Rev. date: 05/04/2022

Dedication

It was very tough to write this book. I don't know even know where to start. There's so much I left out as I just don't have the time to really put into detail, word for word, what really happened. It is very heartbreaking to me to come out with this. I don't like making money from people's deaths.

I would be donating money to the family members that lost their loved ones. This is not just about money; this about getting it off my chest after so many years. God bless!

Part 1

The Navy SEAL

Chapter 1

First Blood

When I was born, my grandfather drowned me.

When I was two, he made me eat slugs and dog shit.

When I was three, he made me catch all the lightning bugs in the sky. "Do you see any more lightning bugs?"

When I was four, he made me catch all the frogs in the swamp and rip their legs off.

When I was five, he made me catch all the snakes in the grass and cut their heads off.

When I was six, he made me sleep in the sewers like a tunnel rat.

When I was seven, he made me build a fort. I love that fort so much.

When I was eight, he said to me, "Do you love that fort?"

I said, "Yes, Grandpa."

He said, "You love that fort more than me?"

I said, "No, Grandpa."

He said, "Good. I want you to burn it down."

So I did.

When I was nine, my grandfather said to me, "Do you swear to protect the United States government at all cost?"

I said, "Yes, Grandpa."

He said, "Will you only listen to me and me only, since I am your mentor."

I said, "Yes, Grandpa."

He said, "Good. Now drink this toxic potion that the government gave me. It's going to put a lot of hair on your back."

I said, "What is it?"

He said, "It's wolf steroids, tiger bones, and other types of toxins so when they poison you, you'll live."

I said, "Okay, Grandpa." So I drank the black potion.

He said, "You won't feel good for about four days but until then, raise your right hand and once again swear to serve and to protect United States government at all cost."

I said, "Yes, Grandpa."

He said, "Good, because you're the best of the best. Now you're a Navy SEAL."

Chapter 2

American Badass

The real American badass is my grandfather, First Sergeant Peter Stasso of the Eleventh Airborne of the American Army. My grandfather is one of the founders of the Navy SEALS after Delta Force got decimated in 1962. John F. Kennedy (JFK) backtrack the credentials of the American Army, and my grandfather had the most medals, 120 medals. I only have one.

Now I'm going to tell you a secret about the SEALS. Back in World War II, Hitler was breeding babies in the Lebensborn camps. These babies were special. Before a Navy sailor got on the submarine, Hitler would make them shoot somebody in the head so they can see the pink mist. Once they did that, they got on the submarine. They was not allowed to have any sexual contact with anybody for six months, and they weren't even allowed to jerk off. They were being watched. When they got off the submarine, Hitler matched their blood type with women that lost their fathers from World War I. Out of twenty thousand babies, two thousand of them were born with a special type O negative blood. These babies were the special forces of the Waffen-SS super soldiers, which is the same as a Navy SEAL. One was German; one was American.

My grandfather Peter decoded Hitler's army by their dog tags and background checks and family trees. They found out that the babies that had special abilities had Navy and Army bloodlines, meaning both their mother and father have Army and Navy bloodlines.

Okay, my father, Walter, was first class sailor in Vietnam. My mother's father, Peter, was first class sergeant in World War II. All you need is two people in your family to have those credentials. I have three. My grandmother was married to Peter. My grandmother's brother Rudolph

Lange is the commander of the German army So I have first class sailor from my father, first class sergeant my grandfather Peter. My grandmother's brother was first in his class commander of the German army, who was Hitler's best friend, my great-uncle Rudolph. Back in World War II, they would not let my great-uncle Rudolph fight against Peter Stasso because they were related. Rudolph Lange, my great-uncle, was gassed by the Russians. Using poison gas was against war tactics, but they had no choice as they couldn't get to Hitler, my grandfather told me.

My grandfather fought in Guam verse the Japanese. He wasn't allowed to go against the German army because he was married to Dorothea Lange, who is Rudolph Lange's sister.

Therefore, I have three people in my family tree that were in the military, but it goes way further than that. You have to have Army and Navy bloodline; and you have to have a family member get killed in the war, a family member get hurt in the war; and you have to kill somebody in the war too. Then all those credentials add up. When the government does the background check on your social security number and finds out that you have military background in your family tree, you are pronounced a Navy SEAL at birth.

Jesse "The Body" Ventura was the first Navy SEAL born in America, but when they found out that information, he was already born. The reason why I was so special is because I wasn't born yet, my grandfather set my father up with my mother deliberately, just to prove a point that these babies were special. And my grandfather had something to prove with me. He had very high expectations about me during the intense training.

Chapter 3

Criminal with Honor

In fifth grade, in Ms. William's class, my grandfather and a CIA agent pulled me out of class and said, "Say goodbye to all your friends. Most likely this will be the last time you would see them again." I said goodbye to my best friend, Robert Bartlett, and a couple girls, Carrieanne McQueeney and Diana la Bova. When my grandfather, the CIA agent, and I left the school, they brought me down to the doctor's office to draw my blood samples. The government wanted my blood. But my grandfather and the CIA agent made some kind of deal for me to stay because my mother was freaking out, screaming, "You're not taking my son."

My grandfather said, "He has to go. He's ready now. We need him." My mother freaked out and said, "You're not taking my son anywhere. He's only nine years old."

My grandfather made a deal with the CIA. I don't really know what they did with my blood samples. I heard them talking about cloning and test tube babies at Area 51. They took about six samples. But I was able to stay and go back to school with my friends to live a normal life.

Unfortunately, my grandfather passed away in 1989. On his deathbed, he said to me, "Jason, you're a SEAL. They can never take that away from you. Whatever you do, don't get arrested. Make me proud." The last time I saw my grandfather was at the funeral home.

He never said the word Navy. He always said the word SEAL. Sea Earth air and land.

At such a young age, I really didn't understand where he was really coming from, other than training purposes. All those years training in the backyard with my grandfather, I always knew I was special, different from the other kids.

Then when I was about eighteen years old, I got arrested. I thought I was in deep shit. But they let me go with no charges. When I was leaving the police station, everybody was congratulating me, shaking my hand.

"How you doing? Nice to meet you." I said, "Wow, this is weird. The police actually like me. Something's not right."

Then six months later I get arrested again, this time around my mother's house. They dragged me out in my underwear and brought me on the front lawn in front of thirty police.

The head sheriff said to everybody out loud, "This is what the government calls a SEAL, and he likes to commit crimes. Isn't that correct, Jason."

I said, "I don't know what you're talkin' about. I didn't do anything."

They said, "Well, our best police officer Mr Johnson over there was tracking you, and somehow you lost him, got home, got undressed in your underwear, and went to sleep. So the government must be right that you are the best of the best to avoid all these guys."

I said, "Once again, I don't know what you're talkin' about." The sergeant said, "You know the crime you just committed." He then said, "Okay, everybody, take a real good look at Jason coz according to the government, he's their property and one day this boy might save your life."

The police looked at each other, and the sheriff let me go again. I said, "Wow, this is great. I could do whatever the hell I want and I get away with it. This is awesome. I shit.......oh, that's right, my grandfather made me a SEAL."

So a few years went by, and I must have gotten arrested at least ten times for stupid things like assault, racketeering, and domestic things like that.

But then I was dropping off two prostitutes at an undercover sting operation with my friend Scotty's taxi company, and I get arrested again. They thought I was there pimp. I had to prove to the judge that I was working. The judge said to me,

"So what do we have here? A criminal with honor. Well, the SEALS don't want to help you no more. They said if you did the crime, you must do the time."

So the judge threw me in jail.

I said, "No, you can't do that to me. You got to let me go. I protect this country." The judge said, "You are a criminal with honor. Now go do the time."

So they threw me back in jail.

The police came to me and said, "Listen, the SEALS don't want to help you no more. You're not one of them no more. They informed us that you're a black op now, so if the government needs help they will call you directly. You're not a part of the SEAL team no more you've been put on the sofa, you're just a black op, like a mercenary Hired hand. If the government needs you they will call you. I said they can't do that my grandfather created them he's there forefather. The police said we're going to let you out tomorrow."

I got in trouble so many times and got arrested, but the courts still couldn't deny me who I really am. They still don't know what I actually know. The government put me on the sofa secrets of the federal army. They changed it to a black ops. A SEAL means you are part of a team and black op means that you work alone solo. So I'm a bad SEAL I kind of like it better that way.

Part 2

The New Prince of Darkness

Chapter 1

Purple Heartbroken

After my grandfather passed away, I was totally lost. I lost my sense of direction and focus in life. At that point in high school, I was playing football or baseball, always the captain of the football team and always picked first in gym. I always knew I was different from theother people. As a hobby, for many years, I was playing the drums, singing, writing music for a rock band for fun. I never took it really seriously at a young age. I was always practicing together with Steven Levesque, a guitar player.

My other band members were Erin Vasqueza and Michael Morrison. We were playing in a band called Bad Vibes. It was just a kid band for fun. At the end of high school, the band broke up. Most of them moved away. I got involved with a woman, a very beautiful woman. After high school, we had a baby and was a family for around two years. When she decided to leave me. I was so heartbroken. I was not in sports no more. I always had people depending on me to be a leader, and now nobody wants to be my friend. It felt like everybody just went against me. My ex really hurt me. I was so down, I didn't leave my room for six months, totally upset. She married somebody else and had children with another man; I was so hurt.

One day my old band member Steven Levesque came back to visit me. I called Erin Vasquez, and we all got together again, it was like a small band reunion. I felt so good. I felt alive again, like I had a purpose in life again. Steven was from Canada, so he had to go back because he had family there. Erin moved to Rhode Island. Same thing, he had to go back. So once again, I felt empty in life. I had no band, no girlfriend, no family, no love..

Chapter 2

Good Times Magazine

Feeling really down about myself, I started working at air industries machining corporation as an SPC controller (statistical process controls time studies manager). I was highly stressed out. All numbers hystergraphs upper and lower control limits. Target plus or minus one thousand of an inch specifications. It was a really a tough job, but I ran the whole company by myself. There were hundreds of employees. I had a coworker of mine, a really good friend, Jeff Clace, a top Bridgeport machinist. His father was Mr. Clace Co of McDonald Douglas. We all worked together on the B-2 bombers, on the landing gear throttle mechanism. He was really a talented machinist engineer.

Jeff Clace knew I was feeling really depressed in my life. He knew that I lost my family and my band, so he came to me with a *Good Times* magazine and said, "Hey, Jay, don't feel so down about yourself. Look at these classified ads for drummers, singers...wanted all kinds of musicians."

I looked at the magazine. Instantly, I was hooked. I tried out over three hundred bands in the tristate area of Long Island, New York. It's amazing how many horrible musicians are out there. I found it very difficult to find talented musicians. I hooked up with several bands out of three hundred tryouts in five years. They were very talented bands. I was a vocalist for a band called Torn and an all-female band called Suffrage. I also played in Deadline and a band called LSD (Labyrinth Satan's Dungeon) on drums.

There were around two hundred applicants for vocalist and one hundred for drums. In these several bands I was in, not all were as professional as I wanted them to be. There were always problems. No matter how talented they were, there were always issues on getting to band practice, whether it was drugs or drinking, and there were always something to mess up the band practice like family reasons or financial reasons. It was very difficult to get together and put together a rock band. It cost a lot of money, and it is very time-consuming. It was very difficult when you are dealing with a bunch of drug addicts. So out of several bands, three hundred tryouts in five years, none of them made money. Not one of them made any money, so I knew I had to keep going on to pursue the right situation. I kept saying to myself, "I am the new prince of darkness. One day the whole world will know who I am. I'll become bigger than Ozzy Osbourne. I must keep looking to find a more professional band."

Chapter 3

Singer Wanted for Metallica Tribute Band

Finally, an ad I like from the *Good Times* magazine classified page: "Singer wanted for Metallica tribute band." Right away I thought to myself if they can play Metallica, they can play anything. So I made the phone call on September 1, 2001. A really talented musician by the name of Jeffrey Ingegno answered the phone.

I said, "Hello, my name is J. Lang. I'm interested in trying out your Metallica tribute band for vocals. What instrument do you play?"

Jeffrey said, "I play all the instruments. I'm the music teacher at Dowling College."

I said, "Great. Do you have original music?"

Jeffrey said, "No, we just do tributes. We're looking to make some money in the local bars."

I said, "Well, I'll be willing to sing Metallica and what other songs you want to work on if you guys are willing to work on my original songs, because if you could play Metallica most definitely you can play my original music. If you could play Metallica, you can play anything in my opinion."

Jeff said, "Well, we're going to give everybody a fair try out no matter what. Come down on September 11, 2001. Oh yeah, in the tryout, it would be a good thing if you play guitar too. So you can do backup rhythm."

I said to Jeff, "I really don't play guitar like that. I only play my own original songs. I can't play a guitar for other people's music. I just can't do it for some reason. I only do original songs, but I know I can sing any rock rap metal song."

So Jeff said, "Okay, come down."

Unfortunately, on that day, September 11, 2001, became the worst day of my life. Lots of friends, family, and love ones lost their lives in the tragedy of 9/11. So the band practice got postponed until two days later, September 13, 2001.

I get to Jeff's house at 3 Tulip Lane, Center Moriches, Long Island. I brought along my best friend, Sy bigas, with me. He would always come to my band practices to hang out. I met drummer Peter Zambuto, bass player Derek Stella, and lead guitar player/producer movie director Jeffrey Ingegno. The first day we met, we actually wrote together an original song called "Osama Must Die" inspired by 9/11, which was supposed to be the day we would first meet.

At the band tryout, I said to the band members, "I can show you my original music, but I have to see something original out of you guys before I can show you all my original songs. Do you guys have any other special talents?" Jeffrey brought out some gruesome bloody rock death metal videos of The great Kat that he made and other rock bands, Slipknot and Kathleen Thomas Beethoven on speed.

In the video, there were some gruesome murders going on. I said to my friend Sy, "Damn, that looks real." Then I sad to Jeffrey, "Is that real because how did you come up with that kind of fake production?" Jeffrey replied, "They are my masterpieces."

He showed us a couple videos that he made. They were death metal rock videos where somebody gruesomely killed women in the video.

"Looks really real…can't be real," I said to myself.

So the band was formed, and Jeffrey was the leader, which was weird to me because I was always the leader in all my bands. I never thought I would run into somebody that was better than me in music. I really looked up to Jeffrey like a father figure in music. I couldn't believe I found someone that talented, finally, after all these years. Peter and Derek were also really talented musicians. They were all twenty years older than me. We were practicing two or three times a week. We were very serious, very professional. Jeffrey had access to the programs from Dowling College. He ordered them to their budget million-dollar programs to create the MP3 download for the iPods that's one of the reasons why Galen college went out of business he went over the budget?

Jeffrey named the band since he was the leader. He called the band 11k. The k stands for kHz.

Meaning if you hear 11k, you go instantly deaf. You don't hear anything ever again. That's because of the power and loudness of the band; heart-stopping drumbeats; hard-core screaming; singing really brutal music; using seven-string guitars, five-string bass guitars custom-made drum kit, DW drum works (which is Peter's uncle in real life). This band was stacked. We can play every song from every rock band. Truly the most professional band I've ever been in—all because of Jeffrey Ingegno. We had over forty original songs and over a hundred cover songs from a hundred different rock bands playing in and out of clubs all across Long Island and New York's five boroughs. I was relentless in booking shows. I had control over the whole New York underground rock scene. If you were a rock metal band, you didn't play a show unless you played with my band, 11k. People like Jesse Blaze Dee Snider, son from Twisted Sister, opened up for my band. Scott, the engineer son from a band called Vertigo Blue from the Howard Stern Show, opened up for my band because my band controlled the whole rock scene. And it was because of me. I'll admit it, I did strong arm on a lot of bands and a lot of clubs for only working with us, but the one thing I never did was rob any of the bands. I always paid them what they deserved.

My band 11k made over quarter million in two years just from shows, running the door collecting from the owners. We played with some really talented bands across Long Island: a band called Exit 53, Eddie Dome (great friend of mine, great bass player), Mike from Laceration (from Queens, the guy's sick screams). Other bands like Good Little Witch and Tommy (a phenomenal guitar player; and extremely talented musicians—all opened up for my band. As big as we were getting, I still want to be more professional. I still want to be the new prince of darkness. I must continue to pursue more opportunities for my band.

Part 3

Band 11 khz

Chapter 1

iTunes

I was driving on the Long Island Expressway heading eastbound toward Shirley Mastic Beach in my 1972 Impala listening to the AM station on the news about 9/11. On the radio station, they mentioned that scattered remains of a couple of bodies were found in the Pine Barrens of Manorville, which was like four miles away from the rehearsal studio.

I said to myself, "What are the chances that these girls are the girls in the video that Jeff made." I almost pulled over. "Wait a second, something's not right." I just shook my head. "No way, this can't be true. I didn't really know Jeff that well. I only knew him about a year."

I get to band practice, and I mentioned it to Jeff.

I said, "Jeff, are you aware about the couple girls being murdered not too far away from here thrown in the woods by the Pine Barrens?"

The place was right down the tracks over this place. Behind Jeff's house was a train track that led right to the Pine Barrens. I know the area really well. I studied the maps while doing some part-time taxi work around the area. I was pretty familiar with the area, living on Long Island my whole life.

I noticed Jeff right away getting a little nervous. I could sense something about him that wasn't right when I mentioned the bodies found not too far away. You would think somebody would be more aware of the situation considering it was only four miles away, but he didn't seem too concerned about it other than the fact he was a little nervous that I knew or heard about it.

We continued to do band practice, recording MP3 downloads on the Internet, selling our own music as an independent record label called South

Shore Sound Studios, which was Jeff's label. The management company was called Sug White entertainment like a runoff of Sug Knight, the ruthless rapper producer. People in the rock scene used to joke around about me calling me Sug White coz I was just as relentless as him in the rock scene, controlling and managing over one thousand bands, always booking a show at the Kozykabin on Deer Park Avenue. Deer Park was where all the famous cars go to race on the strip. I would be outside on the street singing on top of the bar, booking underage shows for bands to showcase themselves and have a chance to play onstage where they never got the opportunity before.

There was a band from Japan coming in to play a show there, with us in the underground rock scene. The band member from Japan was named Ty. He said to me, "You have access to all these bands. You can very easily sign them to the Internet onto iTunes as a subcontractor and create your own digital download websites and make a fortune." I said, "That's a great idea. Let me talk to Jeff. I know he has the technology to do this because he did it for my band 11kHz, so he should be able to do it for all the bands."

So I went to Jeff and said, "Hey, Jeff, I got a good idea. Why don't I take the thousand bands that I manage and have them signed to a label and subcontract them onto iTunes, so we can take 20 percent of the royalties and become like their manager on the Internet."

Right away Jeff took offense to it, kind of shot the idea down. He said, "That's what I went to school for. That's why I'm a teacher, so that's kind of like my thing." I said, "Yeah, but all the bands listen to me and work for me, so I can very easily let them know and tell them to sign to the label, and we can become partners in this, and I'll continue to do a lot of footwork."

Jeff said no. He was selfish. He said he didn't want to do it, which was a lie. There's big money involved with this. He just wanted to do it by himself.

So a few weeks go by, a couple of bands contacted me, telling me they're being robbed off the Internet from somebody, and they believe it's me. I said no way. I looked into it, but I wasn't sure at the time. Jeff did it under my nose, stabbing me in my back, lying to me, robbing the bands from their royalties through the Internet, creating digital download subcontracting websites like DigStation CD Baby Tunecore, and a whole bunch of subcontracting digital download websites that steal music from the Internet through iTunes Amazon Exedra and makes fake reports, robbing all the bands from the royalties through the music industry.

Frustrated, I told my father because my father was an ex-musician playing keyboards for Doors Tribute Doobie Brothers. Unknown to me, my father went behind my back and went to Jeff to confront him about what he did on the Internet to the bands.

One week later, my father was on his deathbed. He said to me, "I think I was poisoned by Jeff. That's why I'm in this condition. I confronted him about the iTunes scandals."

I said, "Why did you do that? You should have stayed out of it. I'm not really sure if it was him or not. I'm almost a hundred percent, but I'm not sure, so you shouldn't have confronted him unless we know for sure."

My father was suffering. He believed Jeff poisoned with lead glycol in a beer that Jeff gave him. They found lead glycol in my father's bloodstream right before he passed away two weeks later. I just couldn't believe that Jeffrey would do this to my father. Why would Jeff want to poison my father? In disbelief, I said, "This cannot be true, or is it?"

Chapter 2

Manhattan

Still in denial that Jeff poisoned my father and murdered girls in rock videos, I continued to work with him professionally. To pursue the band's success, I tried to set up shows all over New York. I get a phone call from one of my best friend Shawn Fawcett. Shawn just got out of prison. He was in prison for six years for arson. His mom had let his dog out to go to the bathroom on the neighbor's lawn. The neighbor came running out and started his car and ran Shawn's dog over, killing him. So Shawn freaked out and burned the guy's house down. He took the rap and went to prison for six years. After not seeing my best friend for six years, I talked to him on the phone and told him I was going to set up a day, on a weekend, with him and we would go to Manhattan to set up some rock concerts across Manhattan. Once again, I turned to Jeff to be more professional.

I said, "Jeff, what should I do when I get to Manhattan to book some shows for us?" So Jeff made about thirty press kits with CDs pictures, bio, and business cards—really professional press kit. I picked up Shawn on a Friday night, hitting up twenty clubs and TV stations all across Manhattan. The first club we stopped at was CBGB'S, a famous punk rock club. The place is graffited from head to toe, really an amazing place to see. We leave our press kit and continued to move to another club, the pyramid Club. So we stop at is the Pyramid Club off Alphabet Avenue A. Nobody was there, so I left the flyers on the front door for someone to contact us. As we're leaving, there were two gay gentlemen walking together with a baby in a carriage. As we were leaving, they yelled at us and said, "Hey, don't you ever put flyers up on my door like that. It's disrespectful."

I said, "Yeah, but there's a hundred bands flyers here." I feel like it wasn't be a big deal. I apologized.

They said, "We play downstairs in the underground cellar. We will refer your information to the club owner."

I said, "Appreciate it."

And we moved on. Every bar we stopped at, I bought a beer and gave it to Shawn. This way, I can get a chance to talk to the owner. Shawn was shit-faced by the end of the night for drinking so many beers. We continued to pursue more clubs into Saturday, all day. The next club we stopped at was Hogs & Heifers.

I said to Shawn, "I really would want to play at this club. There are a lot of bikers here. They love our music playing for other biker clubs before on Long Island."

As we were walking up to Hogs & Heifers, we saw hundreds of motorcycles lined up down the street. The club was packed. When we walked in the clubShawn nudged me with his elbow and said, "Jay, we got to get out of here right now."

I said, "Why? I really want to play at this club."

He said, "Look at those patches. They are all Hell's Angels."

Being from Brentwood, Long Island, me and Shawn are automatically affiliated with the Pagans, which was the archrivals of the Hell's Angels. Right away I realize we're in trouble and we need to get out of there as soon as possible without being noticed. We definitely escaped death as me and Shawn slip out the back door and got away.

I said, "Well, that's one club we're not playing." Manhattan is such an amazing mysterious place that you just don't know what to expect when you go there.

We went down to the rubble of the Twin Towers just to see the damaged that was caused. Around two years after the 9/11 disaster, it was still a war zone down there.

We continued to pursue other clubs, stopping at Hammerstein Ballroom and television stations USA Network FOX every single place we can possibly stop at. I felt like Axl Rose getting off the bus in the video. "Welcome to the jungle." That's what it felt like when I got out in the middle of Manhattan by B. B. King's. Manhattan is just a really special place. When we stopped at Hammerstein Ballroom, we ran into Faith

Hill and Wyclef. They were hanging out at Hammerstein Ballroom outside their tour bus. We were just bullshitting with them about the music scene.

They seemed pretty fed up with the way the club treats some of the artists. Shawn and I moved on to continue to hand out press kits in different clubs and TV stations all over Manhattan. We stopped at USA Network and dropped off a press kit. After hitting up thirty clubs across Manhattan, we scored and booked two rock shows, one at the Pyramid Club on Alphabet and the other club in Harlem.

Not telling me, Jeff got a call from USA Network about directing and producing some shows on the TV station. Jeff hid the information from me. So the only one that really benefited from this was him after I did the footwork.

He didn't even tell me USA contacted him to create a show called White Collar Criminals. Jeff used me as a villain on episode 14 "Jason Lang." Being greedy and selfish, Jeff fed off my success. He changed his name to Jeff Easter, also directing and producing other movies like True Lies with Arnold Schwarzenegger. Jeff turned into extremely talented director. After finding out this information, I realized Jeff was only really out for himself and was kind of using me as a puppet. I didn't like that, but because he was so professional, I was blinded by the limelight so I let it go and continued to pursue the music industry with Jeff as my partner, at least I think he was.

Chapter 3

Poisoned

I was excited that we hooked up with two gigs in Manhattan, one at the Pyramid Club at the Lower East Side and the other up in Harlem, Upper East Side. I drove out to band practice, happy to tell my band members that we landed a couple shows in Manhattan.

Celebrating, Jeff handed everybody a beer and said, "Cheers."

I never really drank in my life. They were open beers, so I only took a couple of sips.

The next day I went blind. My equilibrium was totally off. My balance, coordination, eyesight—everything was not right. I was now at the mercy of my family to help me get to the doctors to figure out what's wrong with me, but you might as well just walk me to the sharks, trying to get my family to help me. I saw several different doctors about my condition. They all came to the conclusion that I was poisoned. After shooting needles in my eyeballs with steroids to make my eyesight and my equilibrium come back, the doctor prescribed me steroids for my eyeballs and meclizine for my equilibrium. I still can't believe somebody would poison me.

"I don't believe it," I kept saying to myself. "Who would poison me? Why would Jeff poison me?"

Unless he really did what he did on the Internet with those snuff videos, maybe he knows I know something. It's weird because at the time, my cell phone would go from 100 percent to 50 percent charging after I just got done charging it. That means is somebody sending a frequency into your phone, tracking you, listening to your conversations.

I called my band members up and told them I don't know if I could do the show as I could barely walk, talk, or stand up.

I lost everything. I lost my regular job. I had five muscle cars: '66 Mustang. '71 Chevelle, '72 Impala, '76 Camaro, and a '77 Monte Carlo. According to Cypress Hill, you have to have five cars to be a rock star. I had six I also had my band's van too. LOL.

So after losing everything I've ever worked for in the music industry, I had to turn to my low-life family members to help me get around. Also, falling back on child support, I lost my license. Everything in my life turned upside down. I was in bed rest for two months. It was only by sheer determination did I get up blind and called my band members and told then I was playing the show in Manhattan. I cannot let this opportunity pass. I would play blind, but I needed someone to pick me up to go into the city.

Jeffrey insisted on picking me up to take me to Manhattan to play the show at the Pyramid Club on Alphabet Avenue in the city. The shows was early in September. It was a bit chilly. Jeffrey picked me up at my house, and as we were driving down Southern State Parkway, he said, "We're going to go past Jones Beach." I was aware that he might be the guy that caused me to go blind by poisoning me. I was very aware of what's going on around me even though I was blind. Remember, I was an ex-SEAL.

So I said to Jeff, "Why are we going that way? It's way out of our way." I know the maps. I know the area. He said, "Well, I want to go past Jones Beach. We're going to be playing there soon."

I said, "Okay, it's your gas."

Driving over Robert Moses Crossway, we started heading westbound on Ocean Parkway toward Gilgo Beach. Jeffrey said, "I have to take a piss." So he pulled over near the dunes at Gilgo Beach. He got out of the car, opened up the back trunk, and pulled out a burlap bag that weighed about sixty to seventy pounds. He walked over and said, "Jay, can you come help me out with this?"

I said, "I could barely see." All I see were blue flashing lights and streaks. I can barely get out of the car and walk. I'm lucky if I can even do this show. I tell Jeff, "I'm blind."

He kind of giggled and said, "Well, just hold the bag with me for a second."

I said, "What is this about, man?"

He said, "Can you help me out for a second?"

So I helped him out and touched the bag. I grabbed it and helped him pick it up.

He then ran it over to the dunes and threw it into the dunes at Gilgo Beach. He jumped back into the car and said, "I know you know what's going on. Now you're involved with it. If I go down for this, you're going down with me."

I said, "I really don't know what the F you're talkin' about. I can barely talk. I can barely see. I'm lucky if I am able to sing to do this show."

So he handed me water. I didn't drink it because I was nervous that this guy would poison me. After that, I didn't know what to believe with this guy.

So we continued to drive on Ocean Parkway at Gilgo, then to Manhattan. We arrived at the Pyramid Club. It's an underground cellar under the streets on Alphabet Avenue. There was a big festival at the park up the road. There were thousands of people all over the place, in the streets, everywhere. It was an amazing scene.

Being blind, people patted me on my back. Onstage, I let them know I was blind. It was the first time that I was performing blind in a show like this. A beautiful woman by the name of Christine—the singer of the band called Ripe, a pop band, very talented—came to visit me. Christine didn't know I went blind. After we played the show, we hang out. I know how beautiful she is because I remembered how she looked. Because I was blind, I didn't really get to hang out too much with her after the show. I walked her to her car. Derek Stella, my bass player, followed me because he knew I was not in good shape. I can't believe I did not go home with this woman. If I wasn't blind, I definitely would have went home with Christine. When the opportunity comes, you best go running.

So after the show, thousands of people congratulated me through the streets of Manhattan. People I don't even know were telling me they saw Metallica and Slayer live several times and only saw me play once and I was blind. They said I was the most powerful singer they've ever seen. "Your band destroys Metallica and Slayer, and we can't believe that you are from Long Island."

Hearing that from people was the greatest feeling in my entire life, because all my life, that was all I ever wanted to be, to be better than my idols.

I noticed that Jeff was very distant that night. I don't think he can believe I played in the condition I was in My equilibrium was totally off, but I still pulled it out only because of sheer determination.

Jeff and I left Manhattan and stopped at Arby's, talking about the show.

I mentioned to him, "What was that whole thing back there by Gilgo Beach? I can't really see too well. What was that all about?"

He said, "Don't worry about it."

I thought, *Did this guy really poison me? Did he really kill my father?*

Still out of disbelief, I continued to work with Jeff but with extreme caution coz at this point I didn't really know if this guy was a narcissist sociopath.

Part 4

There's a Serial Killer among Us

Chapter 1

Imposter

Still in the condition that I was in, we finish out our last show in Manhattan, which was a bust. It was in Black Orchard, a bar in Harlem. I was definitely the backbone of the band, the workhorse footwork. I didn't book any more shows for the next few months. I felt like I needed to take care of my health. It was the first time in my life I turned away from music.

Telling my band members, said I needed to take it easy for a little while so I can get back my health. The band immediately started to fall apart. All my band members were about fifteen years older than me. It was tough to keep them motivated.

After stepping away from the music scene for a few months, I started to feel better. I was eating right and exercising, trying to get my health back up, trying to keep my metabolism up. Out of curiosity I scrolled through the Internet. I noticed that there was a fake Jason Lang artist from Canada that was on iTunes. Right away I said, "No way. It can't be another guy with my same name. Possibly, he is from another country. This can't be true. He must be an imposter."

So I called up this fake Jason Lang that sign to iTunes in Canada. I can't get through to anybody. So I tricked them. I send them a fake email address that they don't know and said that I have a big party in the Hamptons, Long Island. I told them I was willing to pay them $10,000 to perform.

They took the bait. I got a phone call from their manager, a woman. Right away, I said, "Will the real Jason Lang be there?"

She said, "Well, the name of the band is Jason Lang."

I said, "Is the singer the real Jason Lang?"

She said, "No."

I asked her, "Is there anybody in the band named Jason Lang?"

She replied, "No."

So I kind of let the cat out of the bag. I replied, "If this guy isn't the real Rockstar Jason Lang from New York. And nobody in the band is named that, then why are you using that name? Are you aware that there's a rock star from New York with the same name?"

She replied, "No, I'm not aware."

I said to the manager, "Do you have any relations with anybody in the band?" She said, "Yes, the singer is my husband."

"Oh, good," I said to the woman. "Do you love your husband?"

She said, "Yes."

I said, "You want to spend the rest of your life with him?"

She said, "Yes. What is this about? I thought you were trying to book a show."

I said, "Well, if you want to live with your husband for the rest of your life, take my advice and quit the band now, because as soon as I feel better, I'm driving up to Canada, and I'm going to beat the living shit out of him. And all the band members, I'm going to put then in the hospital and break their arms and legs. What is the director/producer's name of this band?"

The woman was crying, saying, "Please don't hurt my husband." I said, "Well, stop being an imposter. Who's your producer?" She said, "I do not know his name.

We're just hired hands." I said, "How can you sign a record deal on iTunes with a producer that you don't even know his name? Take my advice and quit because I'm coming up to Canada to meet you face-to- face.

You would meet the real Jason Lang. Are you trying to feed off the success of my name since I'm from New York and you from another country and technically I can't do anything about it because you're from another country, and I can't even sue you?"

She replied, "I'm sorry."

The band mysteriously disappeared. I thought, I thought to myself that's some iTunes scandal. Curiously, I investigated more. I looked at his song list. It's all cover songs from songs that are over thirty years old. Once the material becomes over thirty years old, it's open to the market. You can buy the rights to redo the song. So I noticed that all the songs were cover songs from Michael Jackson, the Police, Exedra. Okay, wow, there was no original material that this artist was playing. Right there, I know he was an imposter. Then I thought about it more. Jeffrey has no originality. He only does cover songs. In majority of all his material, Jeffrey is really just a cover band. I'm the one with all the originality. Right then, I suspected that Jeffrey ingego produced this fake artist on iTunes to feed off my success.

I thought, *Wow, he's trying to poison me and then take over my name in Canada.*

I called Jeff and said, "There's a fake Jason Lang on iTunes. Did you create this? Tell me the truth."

Jeff replied, "No."

He was lying; I could sense it.

I said, "Well, Jeff, I hope you're right because I'm going up to Canada. I'm going to put him in the hospital."

Jeff knew I am not one to mess with. Being an ex-SEAL, I am extremely tough. Jeff had seen me beat people up many times at the bars. He knew I would go up there and do that.

Like I said earlier, the band mysteriously disappeared.

I told Jeff, "I feel a lot better, so now I'm going to book some more shows. So call the boys up and tell them let's get together. I am ready to play out again."

Chapter 2

Breakup

Derek Stella, my bass player, was twenty years older than me. Now I understand why he had such a hard time getting around when he got older. Derek's wife, Diane, had some complications; so he stepped away from the band for a few weeks.

During the band practice, Jeffrey asked me, "Should we bring Michael Keller as a backup bass player so we can book some shows."

I said, "Michael Keller, the classical musician you work with out in the Hamptons performing classical music romantically at dinners? Jeff, how is Michael Keller going to learn all the material within a few weeks?"

Jeff said, "We're only going to play ten songs. Don't worry, he's a better musician than me."

I said, "No way."

I couldn't believe this. So Michael Keller came to practice and played all the material and learned it in one night. I couldn't believe it. I thought Jeffrey was extremely talented, but Michael Keller was a classical guitar teacher, an amazing musician.

So I landed gigs, one at the Red Zone on Woodside Avenue, Queens. The other show was on Halloween at the Chili Peppers Pub in Mastic Beach, Long Island, which was our band, 11k's backyard.

The first show was at the Red Zone, where the Beastie Boys and the Ramones had their first show. Since they're from the area, they are idols of mine.

I noticed Michael Keller was talking to a woman at the bar, and I overheard Jeff say to him, "She's not the one." I didn't really think much of it. I thought he was just trying to take her home for sex, though that was weird, considering they were both married.

So we played the show, and the first night he played with us, Michael Keller broke Jeffries $2,000 bass guitar on the floor because he think he's a rock star. Meanwhile, I think we only made like $200 from the show. LOL.

The next show at Chili Peppers in Mastic Beach, Long Island, Derek Stella was able to play the show. So I remember that night like the back of my hand. It was dark, foggy, cold night. The place was packed. Everybody was dressed up in devil/evil costumes.

I come onstage and said, "Welcome to my world my world of darkness. When I sing, the ground shakes, the sky closes up, rivers will run red."

The place erupted into a massive mosh pit, fights broke out, people were getting beat up throughout the bar with pool sticks, glass windows were being smashed with bottles. It was one of the best shows I've ever had in my life.

In the middle of the show, one of my friends got into a fight with a family member of my bass player, Derek, by accident in the midst of all the ruckus from the mosh pit. Derek and my drummer, Peter, had enough. They wanted to quit.

I said, "No problem. Nobody's getting paid tonight." I took the whole door cover, over $1,000 in cash. I gave Jeff his cut. The band officially broke up.

Chapter 3

Infiltrate

After the breakup with 11k, I started to work with other bands on side projects in the local rock scene. I hook up with Tommy, lead guitar player for Good Little Witch and the band Permanent Scar. Tommy was an extremely talented guitar player, just as good as Jeff. Tommy and I created a side project called Vicious Cycle. We only made like two songs.

Tommy said, "Permanent Scars is playing at Grizzly Sports Bar in Bayshore. Do you want to come down and perform those songs. I think it would be kind of cool, like a shock to the crowd."

"All right, I'll come down and play couple songs with you guys. Sounds like fun."

*****

I hung out at Grizzly Sports Bar at Bayshore, Long Island. I got onstage, and they announced out loud, "Jason Lang is going to come up onstage and perform a couple songs with Permanent Scar, which is a new band called Vicious Cycle."

The band performed. Sounded really good. Everybody cheered. Everything was great.

I came off the stage to go hang out in the parking lot. Then thirty people came up to me, three different bands.

I said, "Hey, what's up guys? You want my autograph?"

One of them said, "We should beat the s*** out of you right now."

I said, "Back up, man. I don't even know who you are? What's this is about? Back up."

He was a young kid, around eighteen to twenty years old.

He said, "What are you going to do? There's thirty of us."

Being an ex-SEAL black op, I am not afraid to fight thirty people. I have done this before, so I told all of them, "Back up, or I'm going to f*** all of you up. I don't even know who you are, or what this is about?"

One band member said, "There's three bands here."

They all said, "Jason Lang robbed us on iTunes."

I said, "Hold up, man. I never did anything like that. I would never steal anybody's music like that. You have to believe me."

They said, "We don't believe you."

I said, "Listen, why would I show up here at this show knowing that I robbed you guys. Wouldn't that be kind of stupid? Why would I even show my face ever? Why would I come up onstage, say my name out loud, and then rob bands on iTunes. Does that make any sense?"

One kid said, "For some reason, I believe you."

I said, "Explain to me what exactly happened with your music on the Internet through iTunes."

He said, "Jason Lang sent us emails, saying, 'Sign to CD Baby and we will subcontract you on to iTunes to become your management. They take 20 percent and pay the bands out of their royalties after iTunes takes their cut and CD Baby."

I said, "So they sent you an email saying it was me, and then you sign your music to the Internet to somebody you don't even know, and now you think it's me, and you guys want to kill me."

He said, "Yes."

I said, "Well, I'll fight all thirty of you right now if you want, but I'm telling you right now, I did not rob you on iTunes. It sounds like a scandal, and I really think I know who did this. Please let me look into this. I think I know who did this. I believe it is my old guitar player/producer Jeffrey. Give me a few weeks and I'll get back to you guys. I'll contact one of the bands. If I need your help, I'll let you guys know." Then I pulled out $100 bill and said, "Here, this is proof that I'm not lying to you."

He did not take my money. He said that he believed me.

I left Grizzly Sports Bar thinking, *This happened quite a few years ago when other bands told me I was robbing them on iTunes and other subcontracting digital download websites. Also, this other fake Jason Lang from Canada. Did Jeff really do all these things, poisoning me to control the iTunes behind my back?*

There's an old American saying: greed will get you caught. Two weeks before this, I was playing a poker game with gang members of LOD (Legion of Doom), a Black gang. I used to play football with these guys. They were friends of mine. In the poker game, there were three rappers. One was the producer. These rappers were horrible. They all were signed to iTunes, It was their producer that signed them to iTunes. They were all at the poker table rapping against each other.

I said to myself, "If these guys are signed to iTunes and I'm not and now these band members are telling me that somebody's robbing them on iTunes using my name, this got to be Jeff."

So I infiltrated the situation, going undercover. I didn't tell Jeff that I knew about the bands that he was robbing on iTunes using my name. I tried to call Jeff's house several times. No answer. So I drove out to my old band's practice place at Jeffrey's house. When I got there, the house was leveled, and they were putting up a brand-new house with an indoor pool. I said, "What the hell's going on here? This cannot be off a teacher's salary. Something is definitely up here. He must have made a lot of money off this iTunes scandals."

I noticed a trailer on the side of the property. I knocked on the trailer, and it was Kari, Jeff's wife. She came out. She was so happy to see me. She thinks that me and Jeff are big rock stars and I'm probably the good reason why Jeffrey is successful in the music industry. She knew I was a big part of that. This was a great woman. She'd cooked me dinner more than her husband. I knew Carrie had nothing to do with this, so I didn't really want to hurt her feelings and tell her that her husband is a sociopath.

I said, "Kari, you have to get in contact with Jeff. I must talk to him. I want to work with him on a solo project." She contacted Jeffrey.

I got on the phone and said, "Jeff, I've been calling you several times. Why haven't you answered?" He said, "I don't work for you."

I laughed and said, "I need to get together with you. I want to put together a solo project on iTunes. I know you can do it." He said, "I'm too busy

I said, "Well, you better make some time. I was hoping you can make me some videos with some girls in it. I'm not leaving your house until you set up a time that. We can get together to create these solo project on iTunes."

We set up a date to make a solo project, which was just a cover-up so that I can infiltrate the situation. I asked Kari before I left what Jeff was doing in Manhattan. She said that he's working with USA Network on a directing project. I left Jeffrey's house. Curious, I went on the Internet and just scrolled USA Network shows.

I find the show with Michael Keller in it and Jason Lang as villains in the hot TV show White Collar Criminals, another imposter on the Internet, WTF!

Part 5

The Craigslist Ripper

Chapter 1

Gilgo Beach Murderers

I set up a solo project with Jeffrey to try to get more information out of him. I know I have to be extremely cautious, with everything that's going on around me, dealing with a narcissist. I showed up at the studio, year 2009. I knocked on the garage door. The house was still being worked on.

With all the new construction that was going on, the place was a mess. I said, "Jeff, how are we going to record a solo CD for iTunes when this place is a mess."

He started to clean up the area so we can start recording. I said, "Jeff, we're going to sign to iTunes and make millions. I got thousands of people that know me all over the world on Facebook. With Facebook and Twitter social media, this should go big."

I thought Jeff fell for it, but I was not sure. I was still being very cautious about things.

Jeffrey constantly canceled every other week to prolong the CD release on iTunes.

The solo project on iTunes is called "Jason Lang's Unlawful Gathering, the New Prince of Darkness." You can check iTunes that's right there is no more iTunes because of all the iTunes scandals it gave Apple a bad reputation so they had to change the name to Apple music. Right now you can look it up, on Apple music and Amazon music but don't buy it because I don't get the royalties.

Anyway, Jeff always had an excuse not to get together to finish this solo project. Finally, he called me and said, "Let's get together this week." I thought, that is weird because he's been blowing me off like crazy. I was getting really angry thinking that this guy has done all these crazy things to hurt me and my family and my friends. I was hiding a small Carpenters hammer in the back of my pocket. Just in case things get out of hand, I'm going to crack this guy right in his head.

So I went to band practice. Jeffrey didn't tell me he was expecting company. There was a knock on the door. It was Michael Keller, my backup bass player. Jeffrey and he have a side project doing classical guitar music, making money out in the Hamptons. I really like Michael Keller, never had a problem with him. He broke Jeff's bass guitar at the rock show. I thought Jeff was angry at him. I know he tried to pick up that woman at the bar knowing that he was married.

When he came in, I took full caution because now I know it was two versus one. Michael Keller said to me, "Hey, Jason, I came by to hang out with you guys."

I said, "No offense, I really just wanted to work alone with Jeffrey with this solo project we're going to put on iTunes." Michael Keller replied, "That's awesome. I have my music on iTunes. I put my own music on iTunes, and I'm doing really well. When I perform classical guitar at the restaurant, everybody buys the iTunes. I make a killing."

I said, "That's really awesome, Keller. I can't wait to finish this CD." Michael Kelly said, "Jeffrey tells me you have a photographic memory, that you can remember pages of pages upon lyrics." I didn't want Keller to know what abilities I have, so I lied to him and played dumb. I said, "Yeah, I forget sometimes. I mess up all the time." I try to cover it up. Jeffrey looked at me. He knew I never mess up.

Keller said to Jeffrey, "Show Jason the pictures of the four girls on the Internet." Jeffrey brought up the four girls that were murdered in the rock snuff videos that Jeffrey created. Now I came to the conclusion that Jeffrey and Keller made them, which means they are the Craigslist ripper and the Gilgo Beach murderer. Right there, when I saw those pictures, I knew I was in deep trouble. I was ready to grab the hammer out of my back pocket to crack both of these guys in the head, in case they try to mess with me. I am a really good actor, so I said to Jeffrey and Michael, "No, I don't know these girls. I have never seen them before at all."

Jeffrey knew I have a photographic memory. He knew I can remember pages and pages of music by heart and that I can play thousands of songs by ear. He knew of my capabilities. He knew I was lying.

Michael Keller said, "Okay, that's all I need to see."

Michael Keller believed me, but Jeffrey knew me much better than Michael. With sheer caution, I demanded that Jeffrey sign the CD to iTunes.

Chapter 2

White Collar Payback after Michael Keller Left the Rehearsal Studio

I started to think back, getting really angry and upset. I went back on the Internet to investigate this *White Collar Criminal* TV show on USA Network. On episode 14, "White Collar Payback," there was a Jason Lang villain and also a Michael Keller, who was the number one villain on the TV show. This cannot be a coincidence. I thought back when me and my best friend, Shawn Fawcett, went to Manhattan to book all those shows. We walked right to USA Network and handed the executive a press kit. Jeffrey must have gotten the call back without telling me, once again feeding off my success, feeding off my footwork.

I was getting extremely angry, but I still must stay focused and be aware of everything that's around me. I was being well aware of everything that was around me at the studio, but I still carried a small carpenter's hammer in my back pocket waiting for the right moment to crack this guy upside his head. It's either kill him or turn him into the FBI. I keep getting these voices, "Just kill him, just kill him. The world will be a better place. You're an ex-SEAL. They won't hold you in jail for that long."

I tried to keep my composure and finish the CD on iTunes to see exactly what this guy was going to do. Finally on May 1, 2010, which is the anniversary of the Gilgo Beach murders, Jeffrey decided to release the CD on that date. It must be some kind of sick serial killer game he likes to play.

Before we signed to iTunes, Jeffrey said, "You must sign to CD Baby first and then CD Baby will go over the music, correct it, and then sign it to iTunes if they feel like it's worth it."

I knew he was full of s***. They sign anything on iTunes, so I said, "I don't know who CD Baby is. I have to look into this and see who the owner is. Are you sure you don't have anything to do with CD Baby, Jeffrey."

He said, "No."

He was lying. So I investigated CD Baby. I cannot get in touch with anybody from their company.

I went back to Jeffrey and said, "I don't know who this person is. I really don't want to sign my music to them."

Jeffrey said, "Well, if you want to get signed to iTunes, you have to sign to this label first."

I said, "Okay, Jeffrey, if you think that's the right move, I trust your professionalism."

So I signed the contract with CD Baby with subcontracts of the music to twenty other digital download websites on iTunes Amazon, Dig Station, TuneCore, on and on with all these subcontracting digital download websites.

I called up Jeffrey.

"Why is my music all over the Internet, on the subcontracting sites that I didn't even sign to?"

Jeff said, "They must have stolen it."

What a crock of shit. So I came up with a great idea. I sat down with my best friend, Shawn Fawcett, to witness me download over twenty CDs for over $200. When I got the receipts back from the emails through iTunes, mysteriously they disappeared right in front of me and Shawn's eyes. I immediately called Jeff and said, "We got to get together. I want to see the reports on CD Baby and iTunes on how much money is in the account."

Chapter 3

FBI vs. KGB

I knew this was probably the last time I was going back to South Shore Sounds Studios. I'm with my best friend, Shawn, debating if I should just kill Jeff. Before I left, I took pictures of four CDs I downloaded on iTunes.

"Shawn, really quick, take pictures of the receipts from the emails before they disappear. This way we have some kind of proof reference."

He then forwarded me the pictures and kept them on his phone as well. So now I have proof when I go to Jeff's studio, which is really my studio too because half of the equipment there is mine— the drums, the lights, et. I left a lot of band equipment there.

As I was heading down to the studio, I was debating if I was just going to kill him. I kept getting these voices.

"Just kill him, just kill him."

I had the carpenter hammer in my back pocket.

I knocked on the studio. When I walked in, he was with two children.

In my mind I said, *How am I going to kill him with his children here?*

Then he sent his children into the next room.

I said, "Jeff, I want to see all the royalties in the reports and how much money is in the account."

Jeff said, "Well, I told you I can only bring up the CD Baby reports. I cannot show you the iTunes report. I don't have them."

I said, "Jeff, I'm not playing around with you. I want to see the iTunes report now. I did not buy the music from CD Baby, I paid for the music on iTunes."

He said, "You have the receipts?"

I said, "Yes. Now show me the reports."

He said once again, "I could only show you the CD Baby reports."

I said, "Okay, Jeff, show me the CD Baby reports."

There was only $9 on them. I pulled out my hammer and cornered Jeff in the studio and said, "Listen, mf, I have proof receipts of over thirty CD downloads and hundreds of people on Facebook. From Indonesia and around the world, people are downloading this CD on iTunes. You're telling me, on CD Baby you only have $9."

He said, "Yes. Please what this is about?"

I said, "You make one move I'm going to crack you upside your head."

Jeff said, "Please I have children."

Being the great actor that I am, I said, "I'll kill your family." Which was a lie. I would not kill his family. I love his wife. I love his kids. But I will kill him. So I said, "Jeff, I don't care about the girls that you made snuff videos of off the Craigslist sex list. I don't really care about all the bands on iTunes that you robbed. I really don't care about the fake Jason Lang you made in Canada and on the USA Network *White Collar Criminals*. But what I do care about is if you poisoned my father and me. So tell me right now. Did you kill my father?"

I was waiting for him to make a move. I was waiting for him to pull out a gun.

He said, "No. You have to believe me. I didn't do anything to your father. He had complications on his own."

I said, "What about me going blind? What about by Gilgo Beach, when you stop by the dunes going to the Pyramid Club?"

He said, "I don't know. What are you talking about? Please, I'll give you whatever you want."

I said to myself, "If I kill him, what will that prove? I'll never be able to clear my name from all the bands that he robbed." So I said to him, "Where's your checkbook? I want $800,000 so I can pay back the bands that you robbed on iTunes using your fake CD Baby subcontracting digital download websites for the last several years."

Jeff said, "How did you come up with that number?"

I said, "Jeff, I'm not here to negotiate. Either you pay me the money right now or going to kill you and your family."

Jeff said, "Okay, how about you come back in three days and I'll give you a million dollars in cash?"

I said, "Jeff, I'm not playing around. I know what you did with the Craigslist ripper. I know Michael Keller is involved with this. I'm telling you right now, Jeff, if you do not show up here three days with a million dollars in cash, I am going to hunt you and your family down and kill all of you. I'm going to call you that day. I'll meet you here at 8:00 p.m. in three days."

So three days go by, and I called Jeff twelve times. Nobody answered. I drove back to the studio, and I sat there and waited. There was nobody in the house, and he didn't show up.

The hunt was on. I looked all over the place for him. He must have fled the country.

Two weeks go by, and I still could find him. Watching the television, they released the four names of the women that were brutally murdered in the Pine Barrens of Manorville, Long Island. There were train tracks right behind Jeffrey's house, which led directly into the woods toward that area. They found human remains at Gilgo Beach that matched up with the body parts from the Pine Barrens.

I thought back of the day going to Manhattan to play the show at the Pyramid Club. While I was blind from being poisoned, Jeff veered off and went down Robert Moses Ocean Parkway toward Jones Beach, Gilgo Beach. I put one and one together, and it made two. I realized that Jeff and Michael Keller were responsible for the Gilgo Beach murders. Together they are the Craigslist ripper.

I said to myself, "Oh, okay, you like to rob bands on iTunes. You lie to use other people's identities to make money off the Internet. But you also like to make snuff videos from sex workers."

I had seen enough, so I went down to the police department, Third Precinct, in Fifth Avenue. I walked into the police department and said, "I know who you looking for. I know who the murderers are from Gilgo Beach."

The police officer said, "You need a psychiatrist."

I said, "No, you have to believe me. I know who committed the murders from the Pine Barrens and Gilgo Beach."

The officer said, "Get out of here before I lock you up and throw you in the psych ward."

I said, "I'm out of here. The police are stupid."

So I went directly down to the FBI. I walked directly into Central Islip, New York. Not one person stopped me. I walked directly into the FBI, and not one person questioned me. I went walking around the whole facility, waiting for somebody to stop me. I asked questions to people, and I said to them that I have some real important information. Nobody knew anything.

I thought, *I could have walked in here with a bomb strap to myself and nobody would have said anything.*

Finally, I ran into somebody and told him, "Listen, I'm here to talk to somebody about some really important information. You need to know I must talk to somebody important here."

He brought me to a room and said, "Hang on, I'll get someone."

This was the FBI. I could have very easily blown the place up. Finally, they called me in the room. I told them that I have real important information about the murders at Gilgo Beach and about a guy on the Internet robbing bands on iTunes, making fake profiles of me and God knows who else he was doing this to.

The FBI agent said, "Hold on, I want to put you on the lie detector test. but before I do that, are you willing to take this truth serum. It's a pill."

"Guess so." So I take this truth serum pill.

The FBI agent said, "Give me fifteen minutes, and I'll be right back. You have to let it work. Don't worry, it's just to see if you get nervous when you do the lie detector test."

The FBI agent came back into the room. I told him everything I have told you in this book.

The FBI agent said, "Okay, here's my number. Give us a callback in about a week or two and will let you know what happens with him."

I said, "Okay, I really appreciate it. I will be giving you a callback in a week. Thank you."

A week went by. I called up the FBI agent.

He said, "I haven't investigated the case enough yet. Call back in another week."

I called back the following week.

The FBI agent said, "Well, I want to thank you for getting our man. Don't worry about seeing him ever again."

I asked, "What you did with him?"

The FBI agent said, "That's confidential information. I cannot tell you." I said, "What about my music? What about my iTunes? What about all the bands that he robbed on iTunes, making fake profiles and snuff videos? How am I going to get all the money back to pay the bands for the damage he caused?"

The agent replied, "Make new music or write a book. Move on with your life. You'll never see him again, I cannot give you any more information, Mr. Lang." He hangs up the phone.

Furious, I didn't know what to do. Not even the FBI wanted to help me. So I went back on the Internet to investigate the situation. I went on Jeffrey's wife's Facebook. Under the comments, it said, "kari, I can't believe I was married to a Russian spy."

There was like thirty of her girlfriends going on there, asking what's going on. She replied on a Facebook, "They took him away, my husband. I believe he's a Russian spy." I saw this and said, "I knew I should just have crack the guy right his head. This piece of shit Russian."

I did a background check on Jeffrey, on his family tree. It turned out his father was a Russian KGB, which would make him a splinter cell, a spy that's born in America from another country. I believe when the FBI investigated, they found him and deported him back to his country of

Russia. That's what they do to illegal immigrants that commit crimes in other countries. But I think the FBI and the KGB made a trade with each other. "You give me my spy, I'll give you your spy." Kind of making a trade with each other, I don't really know. The Craigslist ripper and the Gilgo Beach murders the case has gone cold. There has not been one murder committed since the day I turned them into the FBI.

Part 6

After Life

Chapter 1

iCAB

After getting myself involved with a bunch of serial-killing narcissist sociopaths, I could barely deal with life knowing that my father was possibly murdered. I could not continue doing music no more. I gave up. I can't bear with myself, thinking that I was the reason why my father was not around anymore. Being really upset and depressed, the same way I felt back before I got involved with the music industry, I found myself having a lot of free time. I called up one of my best friends Scotty Salino.

Scotty owned a taxi company for the last thirty years. I worked with Scotty when I was younger to make some extra money to pay child support.

I called him up and said, "Hey, Scott, you got any work for me? I can drive for you now if you want."

He said, "Oh, big rock star wants to drive a taxi now."

I said, "Yeah, just for fun. Make some extra money. Keep my mind off things."

Scotty gave me a couple airport calls and a couple hospital medical calls. I started working part-time for him.

Few weeks went by, and I said, "Scott, you know I had this idea a long time ago. I just never brought it up because I was so busy in the music industry. I didn't know how to make the time to do this idea I got."

Scotty said, "Let's hear it."

I said, "Well, remember when Domino's Pizza came out with 'track the pizza' on the Internet, and then the iPhones came out, and then you can track the pizza on the iPhone? Well, why we don't make an Internet taxi company where we can make the same kind of business. Order the taxi on the Internet track to taxi to your house, and we make an online

Internet taxi company. The same technology of Domino's Pizza has but just taxi work."

Scotty said, "That's a good idea. We'll call it Scotty's Internet taxi."

I said, "No, we really need to make this something different, something that involves the Internet. I have a really good name. I thought about calling it iCAB."

Scotty said, "Well, you can do that on your own. You don't need my company for that. I'm not really interested unless my name is the name of the company."

I said, "Scott, if you don't mind, I would like to start my own business called iCAB, and we'll start using the emails until we can figure out how we can get the technology to create the program to make the app."

Scotty said, "I don't want nothing to do with it. Good luck."

So I get a business license and started my own taxi company on the Internet named iCAB. The first year in business I made more money than my best friend Scotty made in his thirty years working on his own business. It was instantly successful. My business really grew when Hurricane Sandy hit.

There was no gasoline for two weeks. I heard on the radio that there was a gas station that was filled with gasoline but was being blocked by a falling trees out toward the Hamptons. I gather up 10.5 gallon gas cans. I stole eight of them from around my mother's house from all her neighbors. I grabbed a chainsaw and drove out toward the Hamptons and got toward the street with the fallen tree. I start cutting it up and moved the tree out of the way. I was the first one there at the gas station. I filled up 10.5 gallon containers of gasoline and drove back to my mother's house. I give her one can filled with gasoline and one can to all the neighbors. I kept eight cans for myself. Nobody has gasoline. I went up to Babylon train station, and there was a policeman there.

He said, "I demand you to stop. I demand you to take all these nurses to Good Samaritan Hospital because there is nobody out here with any gasoline. I don't even know how you got the gasoline coz the police don't have any."

Once again, the police are stupid. LOL!

I said, "Good, coz that's why I'm out here."

I hook up with a hundred nurses that were going to Good Samaritan

Hospital to take care of all the patients. I got all their numbers and gave them my emails to set up appointments and create a really good Internet online taxi company called iCAB.

I got a call from Capital One bank. They want to set up an appointment with me about my company because it was the third most successful company in New York that year. I went down to Capital One bank in Bayshore, Long Island, by the South Shore Mall. I set up a business meeting with the loan specialist from Capital One bank. When I went to the business meeting, the loan specialist's name was Uber. You already know what's going to happen next.

So I sat down with Uber and told him my idea.

There were six other gentlemen in the room.

I said, "Hello, my name is Jason. I am the CEO of iCab. I would like to look into the technology that Domino's Pizza has, where you can track the pizza on the Internet. Same thing, you can track the taxi so we can start this online taxi company."

Uber said, "Okay, that's a really good idea, but let me look into the technology and see how much it is. We will give you a call back, and I'll set up another business meeting next week."

So I went back to the business meeting, and Uber said to me, "Well, how much money do you have to invest into this?"

I said, "I have $50,000 in the bank through Capital One. I'm willing to invest $3,000."

Uber laughed and said, "Well, Jason, the technology you want has to deal with a satellite, and they would have to work that off the computer."

I said, "Well, we can make a app on the iPhone, and then they can order the taxi through the app. So we need the app, and we need the satellite to make this company iCab on the Internet so they can call me. Same thing, track the pizza, track the taxi. Same concept."

Uber said, "Well, the technology you want is $3 million dollars, and you're the only person in your own company. Therefore, it's against our company's policy to give you this type of loan. How long do you think it will take you to pay it back?"

I said, "Ten years."

Uber said, "No, we can't give you the loan. That's way too long to pay us back, but why don't you let us do this ourselves for Capital One bank, and then you can be the manager of Suffolk County coz we're going to need somebody to manage it."

So one of the gentlemen in the meeting said to Uber, "Weren't you going to make this a food delivery service anyway. That would be Uber Eats."

Uber replied, "Yes, I plan on making this a food delivery service anyway, but Jason already started the iCab Internet taxi service and claims that there is a lot more money involved with it. Isn't that right, Jason?"

I said, "Yeah, well, if you do an airport call, you'll make fifty bucks. If you do a food delivery call, you will probably barely make $5. So yeah, driving around people would be way more profitable, much more liability."

Right away the businessman changed the idea from food delivery to taxi company. It's more profitable.

I said, "Listen, if you guys plan on stealing my idea, I'm going to sue you and Capital One bank."

Uber said, "You can try, but you'll lose. Did you patent your name iCab? I really like your name."

I said, "What? You plan on stealing that too. I had enough of this. I'm leaving."

Uber said, "Before you leave, what was that about the app? What's this thing about an app."

He didn't even know that information. So there's your story about the history of the people that made America. I admit I got the idea from Domino's Pizza. I only want to do it for me and my family, to create a business down in Babylon Village. I did not have the idea to create it for the whole world. The bank had that financially covered.

So there's your story about all the delivery apps. There's your story on how it all started. So you want to know who really messed up? It was Domino's Pizza, because they had the technology before anybody else. All they had to do was change the name to Domino's Doordash Taxi, and they would have had it all. That's why you see the commercials of Domino's. Support your mom-and-pop shop. Don't buy from the apps because they stole the technology from Domino's Pizza, and now they're losing big business in the middle of the night because they were the only delivery service that late, and now everybody's doing it— McDonald's, Burger King, Exedra. All Domino had to do was just think about it for a minute.

They had the technology. They just didn't know how to utilize it until I came along and changed it. My business, iCAB, was the original online Internet taxi company ever created. Uber and Capital One bank stole my idea. Five months after I left the business meeting, Uber came out. I got lawyers to try to sue Uber and Capital One bank, but my lawyers told me,

"Sorry, you're going to losing in court. You did not patent the program before they did."

I said, "I did not have a chance. They did not give me the business loan. I would have been denied anyway. No matter what, they wanted that business. No matter what, they were denying me that loan, no matter what."

My lawyer said, "They got bigger lawyers. We're going to definitely lose. Save your money. He who runs away will live to fight another day."

There's your story. Upset that I got robbed again, still today I run iCab, my own business in New York. I am very successful and happy but still feel empty for some reason. To feel better, I started thinking about opening a business in the entertainment industry.

Chapter 2

Soak the Joker

I thought, *What type of new entertainment business that I would like to start that doesn't have anything to do with music?* Tough decision. So I called up my best friend, Shawn Fawcett.

"Hey, Shawn. I'm going to come by, and we're going to take a ride in my Camaro that is in your garage. Since it's such a beautiful day out, I figured we would take the muscle car to Deer Park Avenue so we can raise some people for fun."

Shawn said, "Okay, cool, Jay. I'll see you when you get here."

I went to Shawn's house and opened up the garage. The whole right side corner panel was smashed in, like somebody crashed into a brick wall. Thousands of dollars' worth of damage was between the quarter panel and the paint job. This car is a ten-second muscle car.

I said, "Shawn, what the hell is going on here? Who did this?"

Shawn said, "I didn't do it."

So I checked the ignition to see if somebody stole the car and put it back, which doesn't make any sense. Why would somebody steal a car and then put it back?

So I said, "Okay, Shawn, hold on. Let me call over your son, Shane. Hey, Shane, come here. Who did this to my car?" I pulled a $20 bill out.

Right away Shane rats on his father and said, "My father did it."

I give Shane the $20, and he ran off.

I said, "Shawn, your son just sold you out for twenty bucks. Now how are you going to pay for the damage you did to my '70s Camaro."

Shawn said, "Please, Jay, I'll pay for the damages. I'll work for iCab and drive for you to pay back the money. How much do you think the damages are?"

There's at least $5,000 in damages. So I said, "Shawn, you will not drive for me. You're a drunk, and I already know you drove the car drunk and crashed it into a wall. So, therefore, give me the keys. You're not allowed to drive the car ever again. I'll take care of the damages, but just let me think about it for a second, and I'll come up with an idea where I can create a business, and you're going to help me run it. And I don't care what this business is, Shawn. You're going to do it and pay me back by working."

Shawn said, "Okay, Jay. I'll do whatever you want, man."

I was really angry that Shawn crashed my car, but I was even angrier that he lied to me. I was just happy that he was safe because he was driving drunk. This car is extremely dangerous. I don't recommend anybody to drive this car but me. He's lucky he's alive. This car does wheelies. So I thought, *What type of business I can create so we can make money to fix this?*

A long time ago the carnival used to come in town once a year, the Mother Caprini. For years a friend of mine, a clown named Soak the Bloke, which means a drunken clown, owned half of the carnival. He was a dunk tank in the carnival of a very famous clown. After the carnival was over, I used to break down the rides—the merry-go-round, the Zipper, salt-and-pepper shaker, whatever rides they wanted us to break down. So after the carnival, Soak the Bloke would pay everybody who was working when we were finish breaking down the rides.

Shawn was there a lot of times because he lives right around the block. He knows who Soak the Bloke is. After the Bloke paid me for the night, he said to me, "Can you get me some smoke?"

I said, "Yeah, I'll be right back."

I had known the Bloke for quite a few years. He was like sixty years old. I was only like sixteen years old.

I said to the Bloke when I gave him the smoke, "Do you mind if I do a carnival dunk tank like the way you're doing it? I wouldn't call it the same thing though. I wouldn't call it Soak the Bloke. I don't want to steal your name. I don't know what I would call it. But maybe in the future, when you retire, I can maybe do this. I think it's kind of cool."

The Bloke said to me, "I'm retiring in two years. I'm sixty years old.

You could do whatever you want. You're going to give me the smoke for free."

I said, "Yeah, I'll give it to you for free. Pay me my salary for the night, and then when you retire, maybe in the future, I would love to start a dunk tank in the carnival for entertainment."

The Bloke took the smoke.

Thirty years went by, and the Bloke passed away. There was no more Soak the Bloke.

So I said, "Okay, I'm going to do this, and I don't care what Shawn says. He doesn't have a choice."

So I purchased a shark tank, and we turn it into a dunk tank for carnivals. I make business cards. I took it seriously and said, "Shawn, you are now Soak the Joker. You're going to be famous. I'm going to start booking carnivals car shows, horse races, anything we can possibly do in the entertainment business. We're going to do everything we can. You're going to get paid every day, and at the end of the day, half the money is going to going back to me to pay for the damage you did on my Camaro until the $5,000 is paid up."

Shawn didn't know what to believe. He knew I don't play around when it comes to the entertainment business. So I started booking carnivals and car shows all over Long Island. The first car show we did was at MacArthur Airport parking lot. I set the dunk tank up in the middle of the parking lot. It took me hours. I started at 4:00 a.m. in the morning. Nobody was there. When everybody showed up, there were thousands and thousands of people staring at Shawn. I dressed him up in a jester costume, a joker costume, and put him in the dunk tank in ninety-eight-degree weather. I got my microphone and speaker and started soliciting to the crowd.

"Step on up. Five dollars, Soak the Joker. Five bucks. Soak the Joker high and dry."

Shawn was drunk in the dunk tank. He started going off, dissing people to get them to want to dunk him. It felt good again to get back into the entertainment business in some kind of way.

This woman approached me. Her name was Shay Punt.

She said, "How you had the dunk tank in the middle of this parking lot with all these people here?"

I said, "A lot of hard work and determination. I filled up six giant garbage cans of water and transported them back and forth to the car show."

She said, "That's amazing. I would love to book you for my son's birthday party."

I said, "I don't think that would be a good idea. The Joker does not do birthday parties for little kids."

Shea said, "Well, how much? Name your price, and my husband will take care of it."

I said, "Listen, lady, I don't care how much money your husband has. The Joker is not appropriate to do children's parties. He probably will not behave. He is a lush. You see him right now cursing. He's drunk dancing around in the dunk tank, cursing. You want that at your son's birthday party."

She said, "Please, name your price."

I said, "Okay, bring your husband over here so I can talk to him."

She said, "He's busy. Can you take a walk to him?"

I said, "Okay."

So I walked up to Frank Punt.

I said, "Your wife says she wants to book Soak the Joker, my dunk tank, at your children's birthday party. I don't know if that's suitable with you. He likes to curse. He's a drunk, and he's a little crazy."

So Frank Punt and me walked up to the dunk tank so he could see it for himself. He started laughing. He said, "This is the greatest thing I've ever seen in my life. How did you get him to get into that costume and put this dunk tank in the middle of MacArthur Airport."

I said, "I built the dunk tank, a lot of hard work. You have a hose at your house? That's half the battle."

He said, "Name your price."

I said, "Okay. Four hours $400 and $100 deposit today."

Frank handed me $100 bill.

I said, "Okay, you got Soak the Joke at your son's birthday party."

I was told by people that I was wasting my time with this dunk tank, but they were absolutely wrong. Me and Shawn do three parties for Frank Punt three years in a row until his son got older. We also did carnivals all over Long Island for two years, having the greatest time of our lives working together with my best friend, Shawn Fawcett, along with his girl, Kelly Claudia, who helped out in the carnivals.

Because of Soak the Joker, I got to meet Frank Punt, who turned out to be one of the greatest men I ever met in my life. Frank Punt changed my life so much since I've met him. I can't thank him enough. He had been like a father figure to me since I lost my father over twenty years ago.

Frank Punt hired me as his personal chauffeur through iCab. Without Soak the Joker, I would have never met him. Sometimes you don't know what to expect when you go out and do something that nobody else have ever tried.

The last day we work Soak the Joke, Shawn Fawcett and I were the carnival in Westbury. People sliced all four of his tires because Shawn was really pissing everybody off, shooting people with water guns in the dunk tank. I still have the dunk tank. I might just bring it back for fun in the future.

Chapter 3

Heavyweight Championship

I was working iCab, driving Frank Punts' two children to taekwondo practice. When we got back, I mentioned to Frank, "I wish I could fight. I love to fight."

Frank said, "Well, let me know when you're ready. I got the connections. I'll set you up with somebody for a fight in kickboxing."

"Really, Frank? That would be great, but I'm forty years old. Who's going to let me fight?"

Frank said, "Don't worry, let me know when you're ready. Start training hard, and in six months or a year, let me know. We'll keep in touch, and I'll set you up with a great fighter/promotor Bobby Campbell."

I said, "Okay, Frank, I'm going to take this real serious."

Frank said, "Okay, SEAL, let's see how hard you could work for this."

So I went into Rocky mode and started training like an animal. I hurt myself in training many times. I was way too hardcore. After six months of intense training, I was in great shape. I was riding bicycle twenty-five miles a day less than forty minutes and jogging around with weights on my legs and my hands, throwing punches and kicks in the streets of Brentwood Bayshore.

"That's it, Frank. I'm ready."

He gave me the number to Bobby Campbell, owner of Jackhammer.

I called Bobby Campbell and said, "Hello, my name is Jason Lang. I'm an ex-Navy SEAL. I'm willing to fight anybody you got. I'm 6 feet, 252 pounds. I'll fight anybody, kickboxing MMA wrestling. Frank Punt gave me your number."

Bobby Campbell said, "Great, I'm setting up a show at Wantagh

Mulcahey's sports arena in around two months. Keep training and I'll set you up a fight with somebody. It's your first fight, so I'll set you up with the amateur fighter like you. It will both be your first fight."

I said, "Thank you. I will keep training. I can't wait."

*****

Bobby Campbell called me back up about two months later and said, "Come down, I'll give you the paperwork. Go to the doctors. Get physical head examined. All the proper paperwork you need to set up this sanctioned fight with the WKA (World Kickboxing Association)."

I got all the proper information Bobby Campbell needed, and I handed it to him.

He said, "Okay, set you up with a fight with a guy by the name of Little Ugly Dude. You both amateurs, should be a good fight. He's around twenty-four years old, and you're forty-two. You passed all the physicals. That's great."

It felt like I was promoting myself and the music industry. My uncle Keith and I started putting fliers up about the fight. "Jason 'the Navy SEAL' Lang vs. Little Ugly Dude." My uncle Keith, my best friend Sy Bigas, and my brother Peter are my managers at the fight.

*****

We're in the back room doing the weigh-ins, and the doctor said, "Where's the oldest guy here? Where is Jason?"

I said, "That's me. What's up?"

He called a meeting with all the fighters. There were like fifty of us.

He said, "Out of all the fighters here, Jason has the greatest heart rate out of everybody and he's the oldest. That don't make any sense, so whatever you young guys are doing with illegal substances, you better stop it now. Jason, what do you do to stay in shape?"

I said, "I ride a bicycle thirty miles a day in forty minutes."

He said, "That's unbelievable."

I said, "Yeah, I do it on the oncoming traffic. I already got hit by a car twice."

After they checked everybody's heart rate and for controlled substances, they canceled my fight because Little Ugly Dude came up with hepatitis C. I was upset because I promoted the fight.

As I was walking out of the arena, almost into my vehicle, Bobby Campbell stopped me and said, "Jason, I'm sorry about your fight being canceled. But Malik Smith, the heavyweight champion's fight got canceled too because the other fighter came up with an illegal controlled substance. Would you be willing to fight Malik Smith today. I understand if you don't because it's your first fight, and this is his tenth fight that he's undefeated."

I said, "Bobby, you know I'm an ex-SEAL. I will fight anybody at any given notice, anytime. The show must go on. Bobby, if Malik Smith is willing to put up the heavyweight championship, if he loses, I'm going to beat the living shit out of him. I'm going to make him eat collard greens through a straw. How old is he?"

Bobby said, "He's twenty."

I said, "Twenty years old, my son's older than him. I'm going to take this kid and put him over my knee and spank him."

So I meet Malik Smith face-to-face before the fight. He's six feet four, and his arms are longer than me. I could sense he was a little nervous. I was twice his age. He agreed to put up the belt. So with one hour's notice, I took the fight for the heavyweight championship of the WKA at Mulcahy's sports arena in Wantagh, Long Island.

We're getting ready, and the music started. It was not even the right music. Already, things were messed up as we head out toward the kickboxing ring. I was with my brother and my best friend, Sy. I started looking around the place. It was packed. There must be at least five thousand people there. This is my first fight. I don't even know the rules. I didn't even read them. I never realized there was so many rules in professional fighting. I don't know if you guys realize this, but Navy SEALS don't fight fair. Professional fighters fight to win the fight, and Navy SEALS fight to kill. There's a big difference, trust me, when there's so many rules involved. I was just going to walk up, step on his foot, chop him in the throat, then pull his tongue out of his face; but they told me that was illegal.

I said, "Damn, what am I going to do? I got to fight straight up. Okay, I'll just bull him." They put us together. We shook hands. The referee said, "Ding, ding. Fight!" I came up and dropped my gloves. I wanted to see how hard this kid can punch.

"You're the heavyweight champion. Give me your best shot, Malik." Bip, boom, bang.

Malik Smith punches me three times as hard as he can and all I did was smile at him. Malik runs away from me in the ring. This would look really bad for Jackhammer Inc. for their best fighter, their heavyweight champion to lose to an amateur fighter. But I'm not an amateur fighter; I'm an ex-SEAL. I love to fight. We went at it. I tried to throw him over the ropes. The rest stopped to fight. Malik caught me off guard. I lost my balance. I get knocked down. I get up. We keep fighting.

Ding, ding.

First round was over.

I said, "Good, I hope I have tired him out. I'm going to do some rope-a-dope like Muhammad Ali."

Second round started. Ding, ding. Malik caught me again. Quite a few times I go down, but I got right back up. In the middle of the second round, Malik Smith kicked me in the balls. They stopped the fight and gave me ten seconds to catch my breath. Now he really pissed me off. The referee started to fight back up. I knocked Malik Smith down.

Ten, nine, eight, seven, six, five, four, three, two, one. He stood back up. I could sense he's wounded, so I attacked him immediately. I was going for the kill. He was saved by the bell.

Ding, ding.

I sat down. Sy said, "You hurt him, man. Take him out, Jay."

Third round started. Ding, ding. I went right after Malik. He was running away from me in the arena. I came up and cornered him. I started giving some body shots because I know he has long arms. I could sense he was tired, so I let him hit me and start to rope-a-dope like Muhammad Ali. The referee stopped the fight. I believe somebody told him to stop the fight because it would be embarrassing for Jackhammer Inc. and

WKA (World Kickboxing Association) that their heavyweight champion would lose to an amateur fighter. It would be an embarrassment to their organization. The referee stopped the fight on TKO, third knockdown rule to end the fight. Way too many rules. If this was a street fight, I would have killed him. I lost the fight but got a chance to fight for the WKA heavyweight championship.

A week went by. I wanted to fight again, but I wanted to do MMA, mixed martial arts so this way I could do some wrestling, my really strong point. I set up a fight with the WBA (World Black Belt Association) up in Poughkeepsie, New York, with a promoter by the name of John. I gave him a call and said, "John, I'll fight the biggest, toughest, ugliest dude you got. I don't care how big and tough he thinks he is."

John said, "Okay, I know this guy David Simba Nieves, a really talented fighter. I'll set you up with this fighter because nobody wants to fight David Simba."

I said, "Bring it on. I love the challenge."

My best friend, Sy, and I drove all the way to Poughkeepsie, New York, to fight. I heard Eminem and skitz Craven was in the crowd. I said, "Damn, they came to see me."

The place was packed. There were ten thousand people. So before the fight, we did the weigh-in. David Simba Nieves weighed in at 364 pounds, which is 100 pounds over the weight class. I weighed in a 252 pounds.

The doctor said, "No, fight's canceled. David is over the weight limit, and due to regulations, we cannot let the fight go on." I said, "No, this fight is definitely going on. I definitely want to beat the shit out of this guy I don't like him. Plus, I drove all the way up here." The doctor said, "Well, you have to sign a waiver."

I said, "Okay, I'll sign the waiver. If I die, nobody's responsible." I signed the waiver, and we started to get ready for the fight. We started to walk toward the octagon. Me and Simba are really big guys. The octagon was too small for us. As we start fighting, the gate opened up, which caused the fight to stop, throwing off my momentum. I kicked David Simba's left kneecap thirty times in a row, breaking my foot. The amateur referee then gets in the way. Simba threw a kick and split my eyeball open. Blood was spitting out everywhere. The referee stopped the fight and said, "There's too much blood coming out. I'm stopping to fight."

I said, "No."

The referee said, "Sorry, I'm stopping the fight." Then he stopped to fight for no reason. I would have definitely continued to fight Simba. He's a fat pig. He couldn't make the weight. If I knew that, I would definitely put on more muscle to 285 pounds, and then I would have beat the living s*** out of him.

We drove back to Long Island with blood all over me. I lost again. I got a phone call from the Navy SEALS.

They said, "Stop using our name."

I said, "Why?"

They said, "You're not one of us anymore. We told you that already. If you make a lot of money fighting, we're going to sue you. You're making us look bad. This is your second fight. You lost, so stop using my name."

I said, "My grandfather created you."

The commander replied, "Your grandfather's been dead for over twenty years. He's not going to save you now. I am in charge, not you. Now stop using our name."

I said, "Okay, I'm going to call myself the German War Machine now." I hung up.

We drove back to Long Island. I have a broken foot. Still trying to train, I hurt myself and dislocated my shoulder.

Bobby Campbell called me up and said, "You want to fight him. Okay, he's on again. I got to fight this week coming up for Little Ugly Dude. He passed the hepatitis C test. He really needs to fight because you have to have three fights to go pro."

I said, "Okay, I'll do it."

I didn't want to tell Bobby that I had a dislocated shoulder and broken foot.

At the fight, I thought the doctors would find out that I was hurt, but I kind of got through the physical. So me and Little Ugly Dude fight.

First round, he kicked me in the balls. Once again, amateur referees. Second round, he kicked me in the balls again.

I said, "That's it. I had enough."

The referees were horrible. He didn't even call any points off, so I walked out of the arena. I was not going to keep fighting fights with those referees or amateurs, and the fights were rigged. They always favor the home team.

Getting to fight for the heavyweight championship was an unbelievable experience and opportunity that I could not turn down even though I lost all three of my fights I still consider myself a winner. I want to rematch Malik, and I definitely want a rematch versus Simba, you fat pig. Anytime, anyplace, both of you. I have to thank Frank Punt and Bobby Campbell for giving me the opportunity to fight. Truly a dream come true. I wish I would have chosen this road a long time ago. But I guess some things happen for a reason

The End

Afterword

I must have left out twenty conspiracies that I did not want to add into this book because I wasn't 100 percent sure if they were correct, so I left them out. I wanted to make sure that the book was 100 percent true. I did not want to put any false information that I wasn't sure about. These other conspiracies are so horrible I really didn't want to add them into the book. There's a lot of reasons why I wrote this book. The number one reason is to clear up my name from all the bands that were robbed. The other reason is, if I told you I wasn't doing it for money, then I would be lying to you. Sometimes things happen for a reason. If I didn't leave the music industry, I would have never created iCab, which created Uber. Because of that, I was financially able to create Soak the Joker. Which gave the opportunity to meet Frank Punt and the opportunity to fight for the heavyweight championship in kickboxing. You don't really know until you try. The people that succeed in life are the ones that don't stop fighting, the ones that have a goal and continue to try to pursue their dreams. You will not see or hear the last of me. I will continue to create, innovate, and invent new ideas. I have a few new ideas that I'm coming out with in the future that nobody else thought of. I'm not going to tell you because you might steal them. LOL. You will know when the time is right. Before I go, I just want to say one more thing: "*Welcome to my world my world of darkness.*" One day the whole world will know who I am!

About the Book

Real-life story about an American badass who joined a heavy metal rock band. One of the members of the rock band is a serial killer, responsible for the Gilgo Beach murders and was the Craigslist ripper, creating snuff videos. Thousands of bands got robbed on iTunes. There's also a twist at the end. He also helped create Uber. Uber created their company from the technology of Domino's Pizza. He created a company called iCab and got robbed from them, showing the world how shady everybody really is.

About the Author

Multi-talented singer-songwriter businessman.

CPSIA information can be obtained
at www.ICGtesting.com
Printed in the USA
BVHW082118300522
638448BV00002B/149